GHOST STORIES

GHOSTS IN BATTLEFIELDS

By Lisa Owings

EPIC

BELLWETHER MEDIA • MINNEAPOLIS, MN

EPIC BOOKS are no ordinary books. They burst with intense action, high-speed heroics, and shadows of the unknown. Are you ready for an Epic adventure?

This edition first published in 2017 by Bellwether Media, Inc.

No part of this publication may be reproduced in whole or in part without written permission of the publisher.
For information regarding permission, write to Bellwether Media, Inc., Attention: Permissions Department,
5357 Penn Avenue South, Minneapolis, MN 55419.

Library of Congress Cataloging-in-Publication Data

Names: Owings, Lisa, author.
Title: Ghosts in Battlefields / by Lisa Owings.
Description: Minneapolis, MN : Bellwether Media, Inc., [2017] | Series: Epic.
   Ghost Stories | Audience: Ages 7-12. | Audience: Grades 2 to 7. |
   Includes bibliographical references and index.
Identifiers: LCCN 2016006426 | ISBN 9781626174269 (hardcover : alk. paper)
Subjects: LCSH: Haunted places–Juvenile literature. | Battlefields–Juvenile
   literature. | Ghosts–Juvenile literature.
Classification: LCC BF1471 .O95 2017 | DDC 133.1/22–dc23
LC record available at http://lccn.loc.gov/2016006426

Printed in the United States of America, North Mankato, MN.

TABLE OF CONTENTS

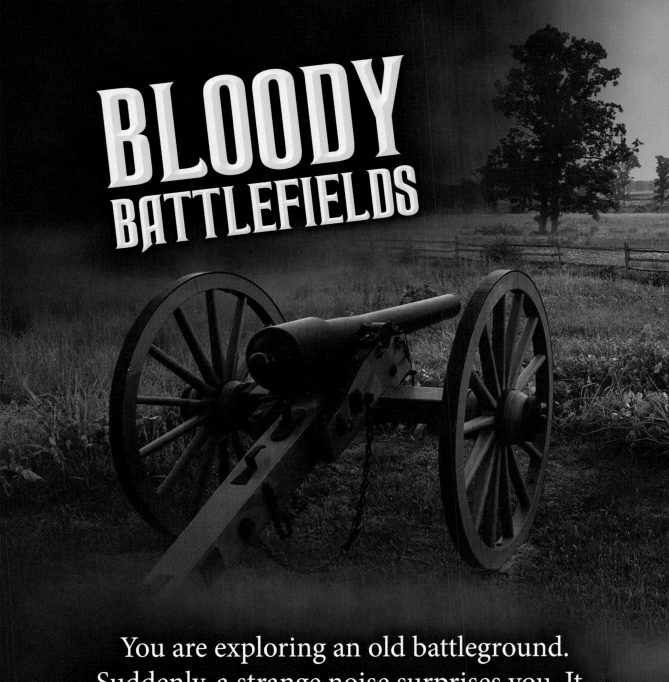

BLOODY BATTLEFIELDS

You are exploring an old battleground. Suddenly, a strange noise surprises you. It sounds like screaming. Could it be a ghost of battles past?

Many brave souls
have died at war. Some
may still haunt the
fields where they fell.

THE GHOST IN THE WINDOW

The Alamo is a **mission** in San Antonio, Texas. It became a battlefield in 1836. There, a small number of Texans fought a large Mexican army. The Texans lost. But they are remembered as heroes.

San Antonio, Texas

Some ghosts of the fallen may still guard the mission.

RESTLESS BONES

Fallen soldiers were buried on the Alamo's grounds. Today's workers often stumble across lost bones.

HISTORY CONNECTION

Texas used to be part of Mexico. Texans fought for and won independence. They shouted, "Remember the Alamo!" in battle.

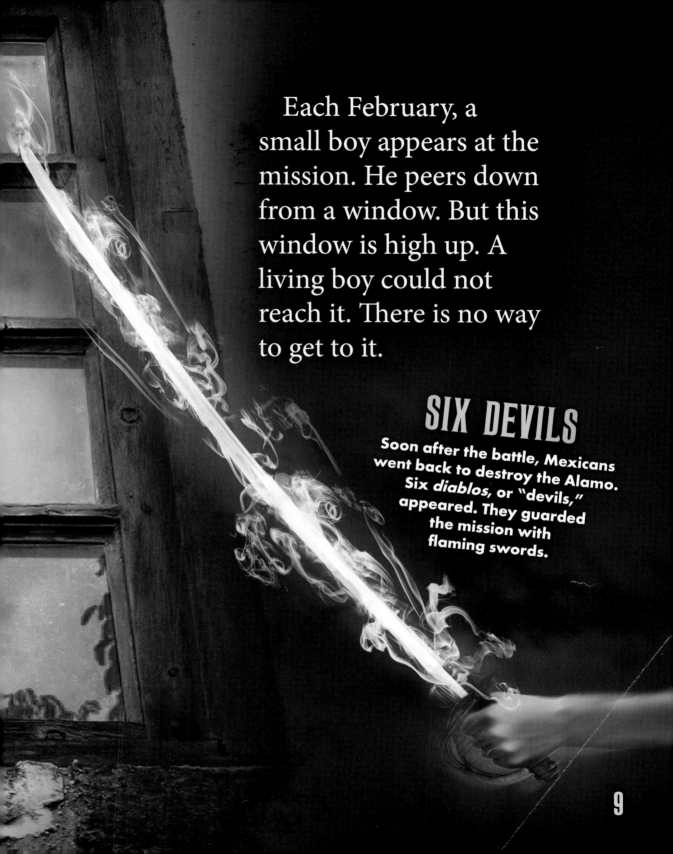

Each February, a small boy appears at the mission. He peers down from a window. But this window is high up. A living boy could not reach it. There is no way to get to it.

SIX DEVILS

Soon after the battle, Mexicans went back to destroy the Alamo. Six *diablos*, or "devils," appeared. They guarded the mission with flaming swords.

Stories say the boy was the son of a soldier. His father died in battle at the Alamo. The boy seems to be looking for someone. Is he waiting for his father's return?

SIGHTINGS AT THE ALAMO

- Six *diablos* with flaming swords
- Sound of horses' hooves each year around the date of battle
- Famous fighter Davy Crockett standing guard
- Ghostly guard walking back and forth atop the Alamo

BULLETS
FROM BEYOND

Gettysburg was the bloodiest battle of the **American Civil War.** Thousands fought and died.

Gettysburg,
Pennsylvania

N
W   E
S

People **reenact** this battle every year.
Even the dead may play a role.

Two reenactors tell a spooky story. A man came up to them on the battlefield. He wore an **authentic** uniform. It smelled of gunpowder.

George Washington's ghost may have helped win Gettysburg. Some say he showed the Union army where to go.

He noted how fierce the battle was. Then he handed the actors bullets.

The bullets looked very old. When the actors looked up, the man was gone.

SIGHTINGS AT GETTYSBURG

- Man appearing on several occasions to show visitors where to go

- Sound of battle cries and horses' hooves

- Battlefield hospital appearing in an old building

- Sound of a ghostly dog howling on the date of his master's death

The bullets were later found to be from 1863. Was the man a true Gettysburg ghost?

WHOSE SIDE ARE YOU ON?

Skeptics think science explains ghost sightings. **Magnetic fields** can make people think they sense ghosts.

FROM BELOW

Some supposedly haunted places sit above magnetic rocks. People argue that ghostly feelings there are actually just magnetic fields.

Ghostly figures could be seen in fog or reflected light. Wind or echoing voices might sound like screams.

Many battlefield visitors are believers.
They think the horror of battle left
an **imprint**.

Can log really look like soldiers in uniform? Perhaps some fighters never left the field!

GLOSSARY

American Civil War—a war between the northern (Union) and southern (Confederate) states that lasted from 1861 to 1865

authentic—real, not copied

imprint—a lasting mark

magnetic fields—spaces around something magnetic in which energy or magnetic forces are noticeable

mission—a building for people who wish to spread their religious faith

reenact—to perform the actions of a past event

skeptics—people who doubt the truth of something

TO LEARN MORE

AT THE LIBRARY

Higgins, Nadia. *Ghosts*. Minneapolis, Minn.: Bellwether Media, 2014.

Pollack, Pam. *What Was the Alamo?* New York, N.Y.: Grosset & Dunlap, 2013.

Tarshis, Lauren. *I Survived the Battle of Gettysburg, 1863*. New York, N.Y.: Scholastic, 2013.

ON THE WEB

Learning more about ghosts in battlefields is as easy as 1, 2, 3.

1. Go to www.factsurfer.com.

2. Enter "ghosts in battlefields" into the search box.

3. Click the "Surf" button and you will see a list of related web sites.

With factsurfer.com, finding more information is just a click away.

INDEX